ADVANCE PRAISE

"The artist working on a canvas may / not own the paintings lying around." This is so true to all true artists and poets. We give all we have to our art that we may not own, cannot afford. Ownership is never the issue for a real artist. Beauty and authenticity are. *Oneness* is a work dedicated to poetry and art, and it's very admirable.

— **Wang Ping**
(Professor Emerita of English, Macalester College, St Paul, Minnesota)

The poems in *Oneness* are extraordinary and insightful. Sengupta takes the reader on a journey of India and beyond. There are rainstorms, good food, and so much more. The poet asks, "Does grief know / its future?" The answer is "Like the river, / it (grief) refuses to cease but / reveals progression." I urge you to read *Oneness* for its vision and sound wisdom.

— **Leah Huete de Maines**
(Poet-in-Residence Emerita at Northern Kentucky University)

ONENESS

Kiriti Sengupta

TRANSCENDENT ZERO PRESS
HOUSTON, TEXAS

Published in the United States of America in March, 2024 by Dustin Pickering and Zachary Weiss, at Transcendent Zero Press, 16429 EL Camino Real Apt. #7, Houston, Texas 77062-5786

Email: Editor@transcendentzeropress.org
Website: www.transcendentzeropress.org

All rights reserved. No part of this publication may be reproduced or transmitted (other than for purposes of review) in any form or by any means, electronic or mechanical, including photocopy, recording, or any information storage and retrieval system without the prior permission in writing from the publisher or the copyright holder where applicable.

Cover Painting: **Samir Mondal** | Details of the Painting: IMPEDIMENT
Actual size: 22 X 15 inches | Year: 1978 | Watercolour on 300gsm Arches paper

Cover Design: **Bitan Chakraborty**

Illustrations: **Pintu Biswas** | Actual size: 8 X 8 inches
Year: 2024 | Acrylic on 300gsm Brustro paper

ISBN-13: 978-1-946460-54-7

Library of Congress Control Number: 2024934538

Copyright © Kiriti Sengupta 2024

Price: US Dollars 12.99 | INR 300/-

for
Prof. Akshaya Kumar
Department of English,
Panjab University, Chandigarh

CONTENTS

Haiku	13–23
Is Winter Back in Delhi?	25
Antara Marwah Walks the Ramp	27
The Man in the Rain	29
Primordial Leaning	31
Savings	33
The Publisher and the Poet	35
On Exit	37
Tenure: Early Years	43
Arrangements	45
Separation	47
Entitlement	49
Equipoise	51

REGALING READERS WITH ONENESS

Kiriti Sengupta, prize-winning poet, translator, editor and publisher, wears many hats. In his latest collection of poems, *Oneness*, he regales readers with an enchanting mix of poetic forms. We have haiku, short poems and even prose pieces. The topics, too, range from gossip and glamour to those with emotional depths. So, we have Antara Marwah walking the ramp and flaunting her baby bump — "She is all smiles as she / treads, flaunting her baby/ bump. The fashion parade / looms large in the new arrival."

This poem of the socialite's juxtaposing the fashion parade with her unborn baby is contrasted with the intensely personal emotions in "On Exit," where Sengupta writes in heart-wrenching words about how the ghee that makes food delicious for him is also smeared on the skin of his father, as the priest assures him that it would make the fire find his "Baba luscious."

The six haiku are lyrical and almost fragile in their selection of words. The sound and sense in them come together as in "full moon / across the landscape / fireflies." There is also covert sarcasm in the haiku in which the poet says that plagiarism tests the memory of the reader.

Oneness is not just worth a read but is also the sort of collection that leads the reader to muse upon what it has offered and find deeper meaning in it. The paintings accompanying the poems add a visual intersection of meaning with the text.

Prof. Nilufer Eruch Bharucha
Co-Director
Mumbai Muenster Institute of Advanced Studies (MMIAS)
University of Mumbai, India

I rived my eyes
for inditing poems.

Would you reckon them
by their length?

haiku

descent of grace
the priest unburdens
the donation box

haiku

full moon
across the landscape
fireflies

haiku

the postbox
recedes to rust
the lost art

haiku

plagiarism
the author examines
the reader's memory

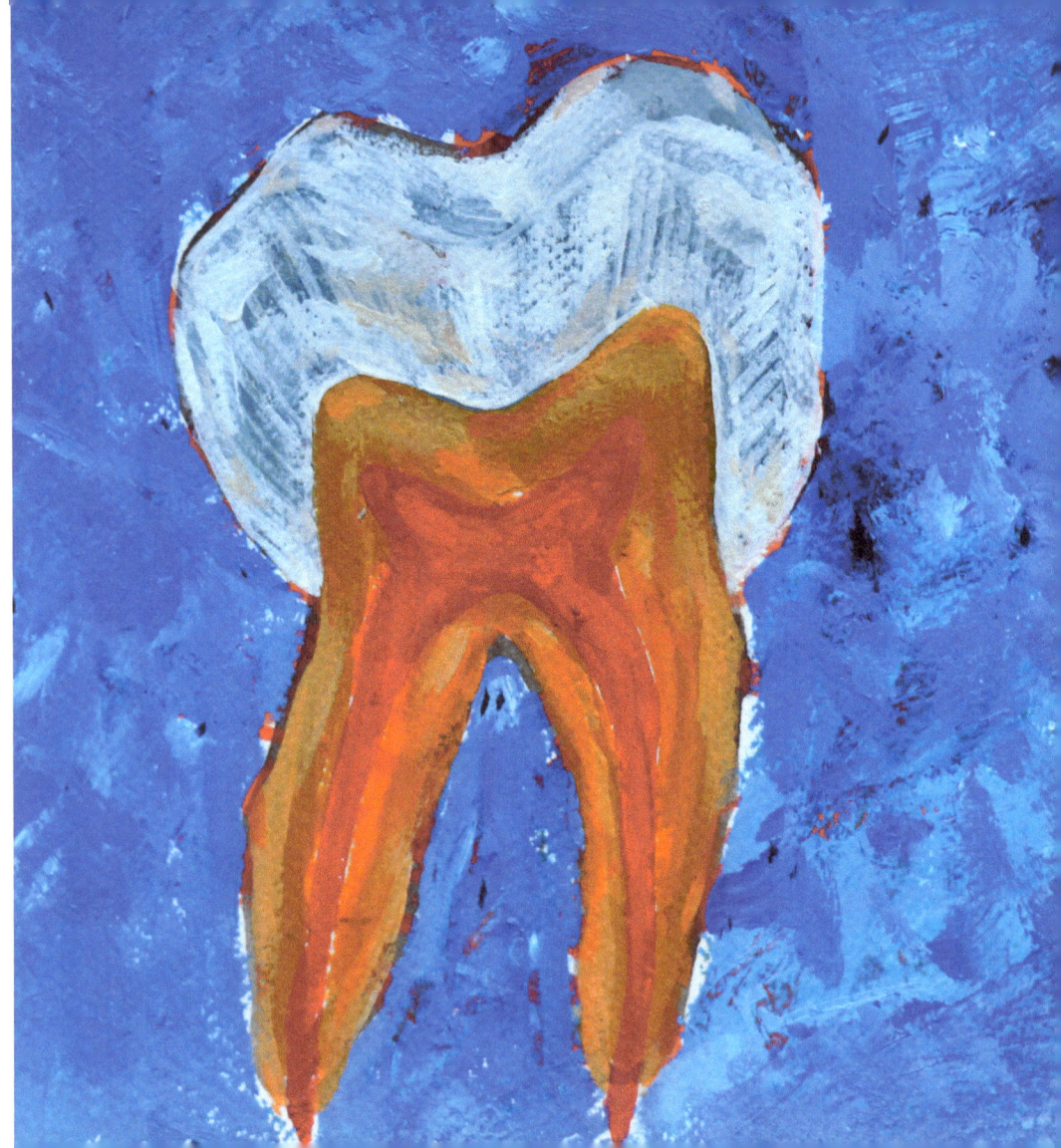

haiku

wisdom
the third molar adds
to the surgeon's expertise

haiku

flowers nestle the landscape
springtide
the poet glimpses it regardless

(Remembering legendary Bengali poet Subhash Mukhopadhyay's iconic coinage—*Flowers bloom or not, it's springtime.*)

Is Winter Back in Delhi?

Cold has an old-world spur to it. I tend to rest more with an inflated appetite. Drops of olive oil on my aging skin add to the impetus. Traditional cuisines cheerfully replace bland meals for the summer. I find warmth in shawls exuding the fragrance of a fabric conditioner. Clean woolens remind me of the quiet season. As the March shower topples the rising temperature, air circulates a frosty shrill. Heat and sweat help me invest myself in work. Will this abrupt climate change make me indulge in the luxuries I cherished in the past few months? Or would the idea of being less fecund engulf me as it does in the downtime?

Antara Marwah Walks the Ramp

She steals the show.
I whisper: *She is*
endearing, isn't she?
I try to spot the choreographer.
What does the model endorse?
What if she had missed a beat?
What if her stilettos broke?
What if...

She is all smiles as she
treads, flaunting her baby
bump. The fashion parade
looms large in the new arrival.

The Man in the Rain

Do I know him?
A man walks down the public road,
ignoring the thunderstorm.
He is alone—
downpour fails to wet him.

The gentleman looks composed.
Seeing him from a distance, I leave
the roadside shade. Incongruity guides
me to approach the stranger.

Drenched in the deluge,
I progress to catch him.
He briskly drifts away.
My cellphone beeps:

The weather forecast suggests
a day-long cloudburst.

Primordial Leaning

You define women as Durga or
Kali. Are you a believer? Are you
being kind? You could have convinced
them to fight the evil. Instead, when you
imply the goddess, do you illustrate
sisterhood with many limbs? Would you
like men to act as Shiva—the destroyer?

Savings

No inner sanctum—it is solid,
keeping relics of Buddha.

Ashoka sowed the stupa with reverence
for the devotees to reap.

Note: The great stupa of Sanchi is in the Raisen district of Madhya Pradesh, India

The Publisher and the Poet

When you admire my piece,
I flash a twinkle.

Unpredicted plaudit alerts
me to explore spam emails.

Submissions don't arrive in
my standard folder anymore.

When you call me a pro,
I notice you are eyeing for

free books you can't claim.
When you designate me

corporate, I catch you curious.
Do you assume the proceeds?

But when you find me impolite,
I sustain your objection.

I appreciate your skill to
navigate my air.

On Exit

1

Does grief know
its future?

Like the river,
it refuses to cease but
reveals progression.

2

Why do I fail
to prefix Late
with my father's name?

3

The family is aware of
my affinity for ghee.
They add a spoonful
to steamed rice, enticing
my appetite.

In the crematorium,
the priest asks me to
smear ghee on my
father's skin. He ensures
the fire finds Baba luscious.

4

When I floated his ashes
in the Ganges, I realized
my father's passage from
his bedroom to the crematory
was therapeutic.

Tenure: Early Years

What role do guardians play
when their wards grow up?

They feed lived experiences,
keep childhood alive.

Juvenescence spans the length
of the parent's life.

Arrangements

Why do we hold the eyes liable
for cognition? Can they glimpse
beyond the story intended for shared
perusal? Visions delude.

The artist working on a canvas may
not own the paintings lying around.

We must realize if other artisans
arrived to display their renditions.

Separation

Only a little needs to be invested
in sketching the worn-out tree.

A charcoal or two, canvas,
and span.

I place myself amid the landscape
to explain the prevailing isolation.

Entitlement

It is sufficient
if you call me Kiriti.
Grandparents bestowed
me with the forename. I wasn't
aware of it until I could talk. I didn't choose
my surname either; my parents weren't my choice.
Pet names insinuate ownership. They work best for the assignors.
It's vital to acquire the right when one desires to name me distinctively.

Equipoise

(for Sreenanda Shankar)

It's interesting to notice
you appreciate restraint.

I noted your claim—
Can't think of a caption…
sometimes silence works.

Your portrait co-occurred,
conveying more than
the penned letters.

Quietude overwhelms.
Pictures register sonic
waves, stemming from
the surface and beneath,
otherwise unheard of.

Kiriti Sengupta, the 2018 Rabindranath Tagore Literary Prize recipient, has poems published in *The Common*, *The Florida Review Online*, *Headway Quarterly*, *Dreich*, *Otoliths*, *Outlook*, *The Chakkar*, and elsewhere. He has authored fourteen books of poetry and prose; two books of translation; and edited nine anthologies. Sengupta is the chief editor of *Ethos Literary Journal*, and he looks after the English language division of *Hawakal Publishers Private Limited*, one of the leading independent presses founded by Bitan Chakraborty. Sengupta lives in New Delhi.

More at www.kiritisengupta.com.

www.ingramcontent.com/pod-product-compliance
Lightning Source LLC
Chambersburg PA
CBHW041725070526
44586CB00001B/6